Alan Ayckbourn, Artistic Director of the Stephen Joseph Theatre, Scarborough, was born in London in 1939. He has written over sixty plays, almost all of which received their first performance at this theatre. Over half have subsequently been produced in the West End, at the Royal National Theatre or the Royal Shakespeare Company. Translated into thirty languages, they have been seen on stage and television throughout the world, receiving many national and international awards. Alan Ayckbourn was appointed a CBE in 1987, and in 1997 received a knighthood for services to the theatre. His book *The Crafty Art of Playmaking* was published by Faber in September 2002.

Denis King was born in Hornchurch, Essex, and began his musical career at the age of six as a banjo-playing singer at children's matinees. By the age of thirteen he was part of 'The King Brothers', one of the most successful pop groups of the 1950s and 60s. When the group disbanded in 1968, he went on to study orchestration at the Guildhall School of Music, London. As a television composer his themes included *Black Beauty*, which won the Ivor Novello award, *We'll Meet Again*, *Hannay*, *Dick Turpin*, *About Face*, *Lovejoy* and *Madson*. He wrote the music for Royal Shakespeare Company's production of *Privates on Parade*, which won the Ivor Novello for Best Musical. Other theatre productions include *Bashville*, *Valentine's Day*, *Lost Empires*, *Treasure Island*, *Worzel Gummidge*, *Wind in the Willows*, *Stepping Out – the Musical*, *A Saint She Ain't,* and *Baby on Board* and *Whenever* (both directed by Alan Ayckbourn).

by the same author

plays
WOMAN IN MIND (DECEMBER BEE)
MR A'S AMAZING MAZE PLAYS
INVISIBLE FRIENDS
THE REVENGERS' COMEDIES
TIME OF MY LIFE
WILDEST DREAMS
COMMUNICATING DOORS
THINGS WE DO FOR LOVE
COMIC POTENTIAL
THE BOY WHO FELL INTO A BOOK
HOUSE AND GARDEN
THE JOLLIES

DAMSELS IN DISTRESS TRILOGY
(*GamePlan, FlatSpin, RolePlay*)

ALAN AYCKBOURN: PLAYS ONE
(*A Chorus of Disapproval, A Small Family Business,
Henceforward . . . , Man of the Moment*)

ALAN AYCKBOURN: PLAYS TWO
(*Ernie's Incredible Illucinations, Invisible Friends,
This Is Where We Came In, My Very Own Story,
The Champion of Paribanou*)

adaptations
THE FOREST by Alexander Ostrovsky

theatre books
THE CRAFTY ART OF PLAYMAKING

ALAN AYCKBOURN

Orvin – Champion of Champions

MUSIC BY DENIS KING

faber and faber

First published in 2003
by Faber and Faber Limited
3 Queen Square, London WC1N 3AU
Published in the United States by Faber and Faber Inc.
an affiliate of Farrar, Straus and Giroux LLC, New York

Typeset by Country Setting, Kingsdown, Kent CT14 8ES
Printed in England by Mackays of Chatham plc, Chatham, Kent

The right of Alan Ayckbourn (words) and Denis King (music)
to be identified as authors of this work has been asserted
in accordance with Section 77 of the Copyright,
Designs and Patents Act 1988

A CIP record for this book
is available from the British Library

ISBN 0-571-22171-8

2 4 6 8 10 9 7 5 3 1

Foreword

I was first approached by the Artistic Director of the National Youth Music Theatre, Jeremy James Taylor, back in 1996 when we both met at one of Andrew Lloyd Webber's convivial Sydmonton Summer Festival bashes where you can, if you're lucky, hear some very good music, consume a lot of excellent wine and as a consequence make rash promises to strangers that you hope they won't hold you to the morning after.

It took Jeremy about five years to remind me of my own rash promise to him but back he came eventually asking if I'd still be interested in writing something original for production by the NYMT. My instinctive reaction was to say sorry but no; that I never write to commission, that I only *ever* these days produce new work for the Stephen Joseph Theatre in Scarborough (which I invariably direct myself) and that, anyway, I think I'd had enough of the writing of musicals to last me the rest of my life.

But Jeremy then added some interesting terms: that there could be a first production in Scarborough, that I could direct it with a composer of my choosing and – to clinch it – that there was a possible maximum cast size of forty-five available. How could a chap say no?

I had recently written a family musical play, *Whenever*, with composer Denis King and felt he might just be intrigued and equally rash enough to consider this proposal a challenge. He agreed and I set off to construct a book which I felt would best address the brief.

At first, it was the sheer scale of the prospective canvas that daunted me. A lifetime of subsidised regional theatre had conditioned me to thinking mainly in cast sizes of five or six or, if we were very good and saved up our actor weeks, of ten maximum. But forty-five? For a start, where was I going to put them all? There was barely room for forty-five actors on our small Scarborough stage to stand; certainly not if we were expecting them to move as well. Well, it would save on a choreographer.

But then I reasoned that although the NYMT has a fine reputation for discovering and developing some of our most exciting young musical and dramatic talent, given that the cast were going to be drawn fifty per cent locally and fifty per cent nationally, there were going to be some who were stronger singers, some who were stronger actors and some, let's face it, who would just be along for a good time, but would be happy to have a go at anything and what's more, get a real buzz out of simply being part of such a venture.

The show, then, became divided into 'principals' – actors who could sing well; 'the choir' – a mixed chorus of singers who could handle the Greek-style narration and thus give the show a strong musical basis and finally the 'crowd' – who sang, danced, acted, fought and generally filled the stage with sound and colour.

I shaped a story filled with complex plot but one which, hopefully, would constantly be moved along with the help of our chorus. There would be a lot of action, thrills and laughs. Generally, there'd be little justification for introducing the songs. Characters would simply sing when they felt like it; and if they didn't feel like it, then they wouldn't – or perhaps because they couldn't, or through circumstances, be unable to.

Orvin is not, you may gather, a work to be taken too seriously. It draws on a wealth of movie inspiration from Olivier's *Hamlet* to Danny Kaye's *The Court Jester* and to the opening of *Gladiator*; from the performances of Woody Allen, Stubby Kaye, Peter Lorre and, one of my own personal heroes, Basil Rathbone.

So it's just a shade eclectic, not to say historic. Much of the material which inspired it was produced long before the young company for whom it is intended would ever have been born. But if it serves to bring them a taste of the joys of that bygone era – long before theatre started to perceive itself as an instrument for grim-faced serious social improvement – when swash was still buckled and sheer fun was still a lofty dramatic ambition to aim for, then these authors will be perfectly content.

Alan Ayckbourn
June 2003

Orvin – Champion of Champions was commissioned by the National Youth Music Theatre and opened at the Stephen Joseph Theatre, Scarborough on 7 August 2003, co-produced by the two companies. The cast was as follows:

Walmund Lee Drage
Ulmar David Moss
Orvin Tim Webb
Prince Dedrick Dominic Tighe
Skeets Simon Eves
Princess Delcine Georgina White
Lord Varian Ben Beechey
Ola Anja Rodford
King Albern Jonathan Scott
Archbishop Jasper Brownrigg
Courtier Jonathan McGovern
Mayor of Zeva Ryan Milne

Celestial Chorus:
Asphodel Gemma Hawkins
Berengaria Chloe Hart
Calista Roxanne Tataei
Disa Lucy Page
Elva Isabel Ramsey
Flavia Freya Brett
Griswold John Sandeman
Hilliard James Benn
Ingmar Owen Visser
Junius Alexander Nicholson
Kenrick Matt Willock
Lathrop Ewan Jones

Courtiers, servants, soldiers, citizens etc.
 led by Aretha Ayeh, Lisa Clifford, Mark Cunningham
 and Joe Tate

 with Harry Baker, Helen Brame, Laura Emerson,
 Luke Fairbotham, Nicola Holliday, Billy Howle,
 Robyn Kilpatrick, Oliver Lewis, Laura Oldfield,
 Lauren Terry and Matthew Tinker

Musical Director Steven Markwick (*keyboards*)
Assistant Musical Director Rebecca Applin‡ (*harp*)

Director Alan Ayckbourn
Composer Denis King
Associate Director Laurie Sansom
Designer Pip Leckenby
Costume Designer Christine Wall
Lighting Designer Kath Geraghty
Fight Director Christopher Main
Choreographer Sheila Carter
Sound Designer Ben Vickers
Senior Stage Manager Dawn Erica Dyson
Deputy Stage Manager Peter Bevan‡
Assistant Stage Managers Tom Nickson*,
 Andrew Patterson*
Assistant to the directors Joe Douglas*
Publicity Assistant Stephanie Smith*

*All of the cast are members of the National Youth Music
Theatre, aged ten to nineteen, as are those marked *.
Those marked ‡ are on the NYMT Training Bursary
Scheme.*

Characters

Ulmar (famous wolf)
a warrior of Sollistis

Orvin (spear friend)
his squire

King Albern (noble warrior)
elderly ruler of Varne

Princess Delcine (sweet and charming)
daughter of Albern

Prince Dedrick (ruler of the people)
Delcine's brother

Lord Varian (changeable)
Delcine's lover

Ola (descendant)
Delcine's maid, later in love with Orvin

Skeets (the swift)
Dedrick's henchman

Walmund (mighty protector)
a warrior of Varne

An Archbishop

A Courtier

The Mayor of Zeva

Courtiers, servants, soldiers, citizens, etc

The Chorus

Women

Asphodel (the wild lily)
Berengaria (spearer of bears)
Calista (most beautiful of women)
Disa (lively spirit)
Elva (friend of the elves)
Flavia (yellow-haired)

Men

Griswold (from the grey forest)
Hilliard (brave in battle)
Ingmar (famous son)
Junius (born in June)
Kenrick (bold ruler)
Lathrop (from the barn farmstead)

Act One

Overture.
As it ends, the stage is in darkness.
From around the auditorium where they are seated, the Chorus sing wordlessly, their voices emerging from the sounds of the orchestra. Finally from the darkness they sing:

Chorus
Gather round,
Good people, gather near,
In order you may hear
The glorious, long-remembered, epic tale –
Of Ulmar, greatest warrior of Sollistis!

Slight pause. The lights start to brighten as dawn breaks.
The stage is empty.

(*softer*) And so their armies met
In a field near Zeva
On the plain of Hypothetica,
Where the two great nations,
The Sollistis and the Varne,
Had come to end
Their long-drawn bitter conflict,
To fight it to the final death.

The music pauses dramatically.
Birdsong. The dawn chorus is under way. Distant dog bark.
From one side of the stage the imposing figure of Walmund, general and leader of the Varne enters.

*He stands unarmed and alone, surveying the field
of battle.*

(*softly*) And first stood Walmund –
Commander of the Varne . . .

*From the other side of the stage the equally impressive
Ulmar enters. He, too, stands quietly alone and
unarmed.*

(*softly*) And then came Ulmar,
Greatest general of Sollistis . . .

*A moment whilst both men stand, apparently unaware
of each other, in the gathering light.*
    As dawn finally breaks, a distant cock crows.
    *Walmund holds out his hand behind him, gesturing
imperiously. A squire trots on and gives him his helmet
and sword. The cock crows again.*
    *Ulmar does the same. No one comes on. He frowns
with displeasure and shakes his head.*

And in the nearby valley,
As the town clock of Zeva did strike the seventh hour –

*A whirring sound as two armoured figures appear.
They are stylised and unreal, the figures on the Zeva
town clock, roughly painted to resemble the colours
of Varne and Sollistis. They move jerkily to meet each
other. They then strike each other's shields alternating
blows with their battle axes, seven strokes in all. The
big clock bell chimes more or less in sync with this.*

And at the seventh and final strike –
(*dramatically*) So did the battle thus begin!

Walmund (*a great battle cry*)
    AAaaaaaaaarrrrgggg!

Ulmar (*likewise*)
    AAaaaaaaaarrrrgggg!

From all directions the two armies come swarming,
the Varne and the Sollistis.
   A musical battle, hand-to-hand fighting. Maybe it
is vocally reinforced by reactions from the chorus –
ooohs, aaahs and cries.
   At the finish, corpses are strewn everywhere. Only
Ulmar and Walmund, exhausted and wounded, are
still standing. Walmund still wears his helmet and
carries his own sword. Ulmar, unhelmeted, has fought
with a 'borrowed' sword. They circle each other.

Chorus (*breathlessly*)
   Aaaaaaahhh!
   And so it has been written,
   That only two remained . . .
   Ulmar of Sollistis
   And Walmund, leader of the mighty Varne . . .

   Musical section.
      Ulmar finds another sword from the ground. The
   two men fight, wearily and cautiously, aware of each
   other's reputation. Finally, Ulmar has Walmund at his
   mercy, mortally wounded and disarmed on the ground.
   Ulmar stands over him, sword raised, about to
   administer the coup de grâce.
      At this point, from behind Ulmar, Orvin, his squire,
   enters. He carries Ulmar's helmet and sword. Orvin is
   short and somewhat overweight. He is very out of
   breath.

   And so it came to pass . . .
   That on this thirteenth day of Ju –

Orvin (*interrupting them, speaking*) My Lord! Your
helmet and sword! I'm sorry, I –

Ulmar (*turning, furious*)
   Orvin! You useless cur!
   I needs should whip you like a do–o–g . . .

3

*Before he can finish, Walmund, taking advantage
of the situation, has drawn his dagger and stabbed
Ulmar fatally. Walmund falls back, his strength spent,
and dies. Ulmar looks surprised. He drops his sword
and staggers about a little, numb with pain and shock.
He stares at Orvin in amazement.*

Orvin (*tentatively*) My Lord . . . ?

Chorus
And so it came to pass . . .
That on this thirteenth day of June,
In the year of the hedgehog . . .
Walmund, leader of the Varne,
Was slain by Ulmar of Sollistis –
The greatest warrior in the –

Ulmar
Orvinnnn, you . . . half . . . wit . . .

*Before they can finish, Ulmar falls dead. Orvin, the
only one left standing, is transfixed with horror.*

Chorus (*trailing off rather feebly*)
– in the kingdom . . .

*Somewhat appalled, Orvin goes to Ulmar and
examines him briefly.*

Orvin (*to himself*) He's dead . . .

Chorus (*softly*)
What has he done?

Orvin (*bemused*) My master's dead!

Chorus
What has he done?
(*loudly, accusingly*) Orvin, what have you done!

*Orvin reacts and becomes aware of them for the first
time. Possibly a light change as well.*

Orvin (*alarmed*) Who the hell are you?

Asphodel We are the Celestial Chorus . . .

Griswold . . . who exist to relate the legends.

Orvin What legends?

Berengaria Legends of courage . . .

Hilliard . . . of bravery in battle . . .

Calista . . . of undying human love . . .

Orvin Where did you spring from? I've never seen you before.

Ingmar We are normally invisible.

Disa Only you can see us now, Orvin.

Orvin Orvin? You know my name?

Chorus Orvin!

Orvin But how –? Why me?

Junius Because you've completely ruined the legend, you fool!

Elva This is the heroic legend of Ulmar the Invincible . . .

Kenrick . . . who, thanks to you, is dead.

Orvin I'm sorry. I – overslept . . . I didn't hear the – cock.

Flavia Didn't hear the –?

Lathrop What sort of excuse is that?

Asphodel You've killed the hero, Orvin.

Orvin I didn't kill him . . . Look, tell you what, why don't we go back to before – before he got killed?

Flavia It's too late now, the telling has begun.

5

Elva
　We have to go on.

Hilliard
　Go on!

Ingmar
　On!

Chorus
　On!

Before Orvin can stop them, the Chorus continue with the recitative.

And so in triumph did bold Ulmar ride –

Orvin　Hey! Hey! Hey! Just a minute –

Chorus　(*ignoring him*)
　To the very gates of Presupposia –

Orvin　(*battling to be heard*) What are you doing?

Chorus
　In the nation of the Var –

Orvin　(*finally stopping them*) Listen! Listen! (*indicating the body*) Ulmar! Dead! Alright! This Ulmar! He dead! Not possible ride in triumph! Horse still alive. But he dead. Alright?

The Chorus stare at him.

(*calming down*) Sorry. I'm sorry. With all respect, you're going to have to start again, aren't you?

Lathrop　We cannot do that.

Berengaria　Once a legend has started –

Asphodel　– it has to run its course.

Ingmar　It needs to be retold, lest humanity forgets.

6

Orvin (*through gritted teeth*) Yes, I can see that. It's just that the hero is dead by the end of verse one. So how are you going to . . .? See my point?

Brief silence.

Hilliard
Meeting!

Disa
Meeting time!

Men
Meeting time!

Women
Meeting time!

Chorus
Meeting time!

The Chorus assemble in a huddle. They do a sort of 'rhubarb', half sung. It's quite quick.

Orvin (*watching them, resignedly*) Oh, for God's sake . . .

Asphodel
Mutter . . . mutter . . . mutter . . . mutter . . . (*etc.*)

Berengaria (*with her*)
Mumble . . . mumble . . . mumble . . . mumble . . . (*etc.*)

Calista (*with them*)
Chatter . . . chatter . . . chatter . . . chatter . . . (*etc.*)

Disa (*with them*)
Murmur . . . murmur . . . murmur . . . murmur . . . (*etc.*)

Elva (*with them*)
Talky . . . talky . . . talky . . . talky . . . (*etc.*)

Flavia (*with them*)
Conversation . . . conversation . . . conversation . . . (*etc.*)

Griswold (*with them*)
Point of order . . . point of order . . . (*etc.*)

Hilliard (*with them*)
Objection . . . objection . . . objection . . . (*etc.*)

Ingmar (*with them*)
I propose we . . . I propose we . . . (*etc.*)

Junius (*with them*)
I second that . . . I second that . . . I second that . . .
    (*etc.*)

Kenrick (*with them*)
All in favour? . . . All in favour? . . . All in favour? . . .
    (*etc.*)

Lathrop (*with them*)
Those against? . . . Those against? . . . Those against?
    (*etc.*)

    Finally:

Chorus (*in unison*)
Agreed!

    The Chorus return to their seats.

Orvin So what are you going to do?

    They ignore him.

Are we cancelling it altogether? Can we all go home,
now?

    Silence.

(*incredulously*) We're not going on?

Flavia It has been agreed that since it was you who
caused this problem –

Elva – you should solve it.

Lathrop We have therefore decided –

8

Kenrick – since Ulmar is dead –

Disa – you will take his place.

Orvin Me? But –

Chorus
   It is agreed.
   And so in triumph did bold Ulmar ride
   To the very gates of Pres –

Orvin Hang on! I can't take his place.

Griswold Why not?

Orvin I can't be Ulmar. He's a – He was a hero! I can't be a hero. I mean, look at me. (*indicating*) Look at me!

Women (*in admiration*) Ooooohhhh!

Orvin Oh, come on . . .

Hilliard No more arguments, wretched squire, it is agreed.

Orvin I'm not doing it, I'm sorry.

Berengaria Are you arguing with us?

Ingmar Arguing with the Celestial Chorus?

Calista We are gods, you know.

Orvin Are you?

Junius Only minor ones . . .

Calista Ssshhh!

Orvin Oh, I didn't realise that.

Disa We can still strike you down, if we choose. Would you not prefer to live your life a hero rather than die a painful, lingering death?

Orvin It probably amounts to the same thing in the long run.

Elva
Take up your helmet and sword and prepare to be
a hero.

Women
Our hero!

Orvin I can't do that!

Men
Our hero!

Orvin I can't even sing!

Chorus
Our hero! Hero! Hero!

Orvin Oh, hell!

Chorus
And so in triumph did bold Ulmar ride,
To the very gates of Presupposia
In the nation of the Varne.

*The battlefield dead are all re-animated during the
next and become a wildly cheering crowd.*

And as he rode through the countryside,
Every farmer, serf and slave
Cheered him to the echo,
Every varlet, every knave,
Crying –

Everyone (*lustily*)
Ulmar! Ulmar!
The way is clear for Ulmar –
Ulmar!
Let's hear a cheer for Ulmar!
Ulmar!
No more to fear with Ulmar!
Ulmar!
Speech! Speech! Speech!

Silence. They all look expectantly at Orvin.

Orvin (*huskily, hesitantly*)
  If you've –

Sorry –

  If you've –

  Pause.

  If you've hit – (*He hesitates.*)

Old Woman (*loudly*) What did he say?

Crowd Ssshhh!

Orvin
  If you've hit rock bottom,
  All the dreams you had have died,
  You're some dated, second-rated also-ran,
  You can always count on me, dear friends,
  To be there by your side,
  When the world seems out to get you,
  I'm your man!

  I'm your man!
  I'm your man!
  Rest assured I'll do the very best I can,
  To see you through.
  You can't hope for no one better,
  Here-on-in and hitherto
  In your very darkest moments,
  I'm your man!

  If you had a problem
  Say, the gods were getting mad
  Like they've always done before the world began,
  I'd be first up there defending you,
  Give everything I had,
  When you're stuffed and trussed and roasted,
  I'm your man.

During the next they help Orvin to buckle on Ulmar's sword and put on his helmet. It is, predictably, far too big for him.

Chorus
He's our man,
He's our man,
Rest assured he'll do the very best he can
To see us through.
We can't hope for no one finer,
Without furthermore ado,
He's our champion, he's our hero,
He's our man!

Orvin (*inaudible under the helmet*)
I'm your man.

Chorus
He's our man.

Orvin (*inaudible under the helmet*)
I'm your man.

Chorus
He's our man.

All
Rest assured he'll do the very best he can
To see us through,

Chorus
You can't hope for no one finer,

Orvin (*inaudible under the helmet*)
I'm the man for me and you –

Chorus
For me and you.

Orvin (*managing to raise the helmet for a split second*)
Every woman I'll protect her,

The helmet slams shut again. He wrestles.

Women
He's our Ulysses, our Hector,

Orvin (*raising the helmet again*)
I'm your champion,

The helmet slams shut again.

Men
Our hero,

All
He's our man!

Orvin (*raising the helmet again*)
I'm your man!

The helmet slams finally shut, apparently jammed tight. Orvin is carried from the stage, shoulder-high, by the exultant crowd.

Chorus
Meanwhile . . .
Deep in the Royal Castle of Presupposia,
In the darkest heart of Varne,
Waited Dedrick . . .

Dramatic chord. Dedrick enters as the scene changes to the Royal Castle at Presupposia. Lots of echoing corridors and torches. It is always dark in Varne.

Brother of Princess Delcine,
Son of Albern,
And pretender to the throne of Varne . . .

Music continues under. Dedrick stands thoughtfully, smiling to himself. This is a quiet, charming, confident villain. No hint of the melodramatic.

Dedrick (*calling softly*) Skeets . . .

Skeets steps from the shadows. He is never far from Dedrick, whom he serves slavishly. A dangerous, treacherous man.

Skeets My Lord?

Dedrick What news?

Skeets Ulmar is approaching, My Lord Dedrick. He is expected presently.

Dedrick Then we must welcome him, Skeets, must we not?

Skeets (*puzzled*) My Lord?

Dedrick Since he is come to wed my sister, the Lady Delcine, we must make my prospective brother-in-law welcome, surely?

Skeets If you say so, My Lord . . . but . . . if they are to be wed . . .?

Dedrick If Ulmar were to wed Delcine what then, you say? On the death of my father Albern, it would be they who rule, not I?

Skeets Undoubtedly, My Lord. For it is decreed that if the elder daughter were to wed before the death of her –

Dedrick *If*, Skeets. *If* my sister were to wed.

Skeets If, My Lord?

Dedrick If. Such a tiny word, is it not?

Skeets You have other plans, My Lord Dedrick?

The music starts to build to an intro of a very big number indeed. Dedrick is about to launch into a major ballad.

Dedrick (*smiling*) Oh, yes, Skeets. Other plans. Other plans, indeed.

Since I was a child, I have dreamt of the day . . .

Delcine (*off, calling*) Brother! Brother!

Dedrick stops.

Dedrick (*frustratedly*) Oh confound it! Later!

Delcine enters. She is very beautiful, at present quite agitated.

Delcine!

Delcine (*she embraces*) Oh, dear brother!

Dedrick (*fondly embracing her*) Dearest sister! What is it that troubles you, my sweet?

Delcine I have just heard that . . . (*She notices Skeets.*)

Dedrick nods to Skeets, who goes, merging into the shadows.

Dedrick Proceed. We are alone, now.

Delcine I have just heard that Ulmar is even now approaching. Our armies have been defeated, Walmund is slain and Ulmar is here to – to –

Dedrick To marry you, sister.

Delcine What am I to do, brother?

Dedrick Delcine, answer me truthfully. Is it your wish that you should marry Ulmar?

Delcine No, brother. A thousand times. You know that I love another.

Dedrick My Lord Varian?

Delcine (*savouring the name*) Varian . . . Varian . . . Varian . . . Oh, simply to hear his name is –

Dedrick Then it is Varian whom you shall marry, my dear.

Delcine But it is decreed that I should marry Ulmar of Sollistis. I cannot go against our father's wishes . . . If I were to do so he would –

Dedrick (*calming her*) Hush! Be calm. I swear to you, Delcine, above all things, nothing is more important to me than my beloved sister's happiness. (*holding both her hands and gazing into her eyes*) I swear it on my life.

Delcine (*moved by this*) Oh, my dearest brother.

A fanfare, off.

But how will you –?

Skeets re-enters, hurriedly.

Skeets My Lord . . .

Dedrick (*breaking from Delcine*) We must prepare. I will see you in the Grand Chamber, sister.

Delcine (*as Dedrick goes, affectionately*) God go with you, brother!

Dedrick leaves with Skeets swiftly. Delcine is about to leave too when Varian enters. Young, passionate, handsome and intense.

Varian Delcine . . .

Delcine (*immediately running to him*) Varian!

Varian Oh, my beloved, I have just heard the news.

Delcine I will not marry him, Varian! I swear I will not marry him. It is you that I love. I will die rather than marry him.

Varian Have no fear. He shall not have you. Whilst I live, no man shall touch you, Delcine, but I. And even I, only after we are wed. I swear it.

Delcine Yes.

Varian I have taken a holy vow, Delcine. I shall not lay a finger upon you until we are wed.

Delcine Well, I think a finger would mean no harm, Varian.

Varian I do not fear this Ulmar. No matter he is said to be seven feet tall and the greatest swordsman in all Sollistis. What care I for his finely muscled body, carved as if from a giant oak . . .

Delcine It is?

Varian I curse his piercing blue eyes and his noble features carved from the very rock itself . . .

Delcine He has?

Varian He shall not touch you, my sweet. I shall face him.

Delcine Dearest Varian, you would fight this – colossus – for me?

Varian If – if necessary I would, yes.

Delcine But, Varian, you faint at the very sight of blood, my love –

Varian (*alarmed, looking around*) Sssh! That must never be known.

Delcine No.

Varian No one else must know it, Delcine. You must tell no one.

Delcine I never will, I promise.

Varian That is my shame and our secret.

Delcine It is our secret, I swear it!

Another fanfare, closer this time.
   Ola, Delcine's young maid, enters.

17

Ola My Lady, you must come quickly . . .

Varian Wait! Delcine! I have written you a new poem . . .
You must hear it.

Delcine Another poem?

Varian I could not contain it. The verses burst from my
breast like notes from a lovesick linnet . . .

Ola (*agitatedly*) Please, sire . . .

Delcine My love, I do not think there is time for a
poem . . .

Varian It is brief, I promise.

Delcine And not too – not too morbid?

Varian Morbid? You find my poetry morbid?

Delcine Just sometimes. A little – poignant.

Varian I thought you loved my poignant poems?

Delcine I do.

Varian Last time you fainted away.

Delcine Yes, I remember doing so.

Varian This one tells only of love, Delcine.

Delcine Oh, well then . . .

Ola My Lady . . .

Delcine Be quiet, girl. I wish to hear the poem.

Varian It is about my love for you, Delcine. It is called –
'Till Death'.

Delcine Oh. (*to Ola*) Stand close behind me.

Varian
   I crave your pardon for my sheer persistence
   But I have little else but love to give –

You are the reason for my mere existence –
Without you I'd have little cause to live . . .
Till death! Till death . . .
My final dying breath –
I'm yours till cabbages take wing,
Till my demise –
Till all within me dies
I'm yours till spiders start to sing . . .

Delcine Oh, that is so beautiful, Varian, thank you.
Now, I really must now be –

Varian There's more!

I love you, Lady, with complete devotion,
I cannot wait for us to sail away,
To start our voyages on love's sweet ocean,
I hunger, thirsting for that precious day,
Till death arrives
And terminates our lives,
Till age has withered us away,
Till all your charms
Have crumbled in my arms,
Till we both moulder and decay –

Delcine (*swaying slightly, to Ola*) My smelling salts!
Quickly!

Ola obliges.

Varian
When in the graveyard we are quietly resting,
People will recall those dying words that we both said
Upon our last and final breath –
Till death! Sweet death!

*Despite the smelling salts, Delcine faints away on the
ground. Ola works to revive her.*

Ola My Lady –

Varian It has happened again. Can mere poetry have such an effect on a human soul?

Ola Yours can indeed, My Lord.

Varian You think so?

Ola It was with difficulty that I stayed upright myself, My Lord.

Varian What? Guard your tongue, girl, and see to your mistress. Or I will . . .

Ola Oh, you would not, sire. Surely?

Varian I might.

Ola Please don't punish me. I am just a poor servant, sire. I am punished enough. Look, this morning I was trimming My Lady's toe nails when the knife slipped and cut my hand. (*showing him*) Look see, here. It still bleeds, sire.

Varian Oh, dear heaven! (*He sways and totters, about to pass out.*)

Ola
  Was there ever quite a couple such as these two?
  Have you ever seen their like in all your life,
  It's very rare that both of them are conscious,
  They will make a simply perfect man and wife.
  How on earth they going to start producing children?
  Quite impossible and, with a bit of luck,
  It'll never get delivered in the first place,
  If the parents never get the chance to –

  Dedrick has re-entered with Skeets, during this last.

(*hastily*) My Lord!

Dedrick What has happened here?

Ola Your pardon, sire.

20

Ola attends to Delcine, who slowly revives.

Dedrick What ails my sister? Should she not be preparing? Why is she still here?

Varian groans and straightens up.

Varian, what troubles you, fellow?

Varian (*straightening up*) Nothing, My Lord Dedrick. I must attend the royal party. Excuse me.

Varian totters off uncertainly. Delcine is being helped to her feet.

Dedrick (*suspiciously*) What has happened here, wench?

Ola I believe it was Lord Varian's poetry, sire. It – overcame My Lady.

Delcine (*still dizzy*) Oh!

Ola Come, My Lady, please! It is time . . .

Dedrick (*gently*) The girl is right. It is time to prepare yourself, sister.

Delcine Very well.

Delcine goes. Varian goes off the other way. Ola is about to follow Delcine.

Dedrick (*calling Ola back*) Girl! Yes, you! Come here! What is your name?

Ola Ola, My Lord.

Dedrick Ola. (*savouring the sound*) Ola! Ola! Ola, I overheard you just now. Tell me, do you normally speak in that tone about your mistress?

Ola I was – I was –

Dedrick (*very close to her*) You have beautiful eyes, my dear.

Ola Thank you, sire.

Dedrick It would be a pity to have them swollen with tears, would it not?

Ola (*faintly*) My Lord?

Dedrick Because if I ever chance to hear you speak of my sister in such manner again, I will have you thrashed within an inch of your life. You understand that?

Ola (*an inaudible squeak*) Sire.

Dedrick (*sharply*) Now, begone!

Ola Sire!

Ola hurries out.

Dedrick (*suddenly all smiles, to Skeets*) On such days, there is nothing more pleasurable, Skeets, than terrifying a serving wench.

Skeets Nothing I can recall.

Another fanfare. Very close now.

Here they come, sire!

Dedrick is deep in thought. The intro music to his song has started.

Sire!

Dedrick (*abstracted*) Mmm?

Skeets If you ever do have her beaten, My Lord, may I be the one to do it?

Dedrick That will entirely depend on your own behaviour, Skeets, will it not?

Dedrick laughs. Skeets smiles.

Since I was a child, I have dreamt of the day . . .

Grand processional music interrupts him.

(*frustratedly*) Oh confound it! Later!

The Chorus rise.

Chorus
Long live the King! Long live the King!
Long, long, long, long – long, live the King!

*The royal party enters. Courtiers, guards, among them
Varian and a resplendent Archbishop. Finally, the
King, Albern, incredibly elderly, frail and hardly with
it at all. On his arm, Delcine. Dedrick takes his place
close to Albern. Skeets blends unobtrusively into the
crowd.*
The fanfares cease. All wait for Albern to speak.

Albern (*feebly*) On this fair day, I greet you all, dear
friends, citizens and – subjects. We are here to welcome
Olwyn –

Dedrick (*softly*) Ulmar . . .

Albern – Alvar – great leader and warrior to our fair
kingdom. We are gathered here to pledge to him in
marriage my beloved daughter – Delcine – so like her
dear late mother in so many ways – in a union designed
to bring together our two great nations, Varne and . . .
and the other one –

Dedrick Sollistis.

Albern The other one, yes. Dear friends all, now
welcome Arthur –

Dedrick Ulmar –

Albern – Olga . . . with our Anthem for a Champion.

The band strike up.
*The anthem is sung, during which Orvin comes on,
ringed by a very tall guard of honour.*

23

All

> The conq'ring champion now returns,
> Who shrugs at fear, who danger spurns,
> Ensures the fire of freedom burns . . .
> We welcome you this day.

The women of the court gasp with delight at the
sudden influx of male pulchritude.

Women Aaaaaah!

All

> This man of rock who stands so tall,
> Before whose sword the guilty fall,
> With giant steps, bestriding all
> We welcome you this day –

The guard parts, standing back to reveal Orvin in his
helmet, now wearing some rather large, ill-fitting
armour.

Women (*somewhat disappointed*) Oh . . .

All

> We welcome you, we welcome you,
> We welcome you this day!

The anthem ends. Orvin remains with his helmet on.

Albern (*a written, prepared speech*) Brave champion,
giant among men – (*to Dedrick*) – is that him?

Dedrick Yes, father –

Albern Good gracious me! Welcome, O seasoned oak!
O colossus of the people, O rock-hewn titan, O mountain
of masculinity, O veritable Goliath – (*to Dedrick*) You
sure it's him –?

Dedrick Apparently, father –

Albern O, true son of Samson . . . (*tiring of all this*) . . .
and so on and so on, we greet you and bid you welcome.

24

Orvin (*from under his helmet, inaudibly*) Hanghoo hery huch.

Albern What? What did he say? Everything that we treasure we now willingly offer to you. And none more dear than my only daughter, the fair Princess Delcine.

Dedrick (*prompting her to step forward*) Delcine!

> *Delcine reluctantly steps forward and kneels in front of Orvin, head bowed. The Archbishop steps forward.*

Archbishop (*prompting Delcine softly*)
I humbly pledge myself to you, My Lord Ulmar.

Delcine (*sullenly*)
I humbly pledge myself to you, My Lord Ulmar.

Orvin (*under the helmet*) Mnneerr moop . . .

Albern (*to Dedrick*) Does he not speak any English at all?

> *One of the escort steps forward and takes off Orvin's helmet.*

Orvin Thank you.

Archbishop (*to Orvin*)
And I in turn do pledge myself to thee, fair one.

Orvin (*staring at him, startled*) What? Who are you? What's your game?

Archbishop (*indicating Delcine*) You say it to her.

And I in turn do pledge myself to thee, fair one.

Orvin (*realising*) Oh, I see!

And I –

Archbishop
– in turn do pledge –

25

Orvin
  – in turn do pledge –

Archbishop
  – myself to thee, fair one –

Orvin
  – myself to thee, fair one.

That doesn't mean I'm married to her now, does it?

Archbishop You have merely pledged yourselves. The wedding is tomorrow. Now, help the lady to her feet. You say, arise!

Orvin Right. Arise!

  Orvin helps Delcine, awkwardly.

  Hello.

Delcine (*lifting her head and seeing Orvin for the first time*) Oh, dear *God*!

  Delcine sways and threatens to swoon. Dedrick moves forward to support her.

Courtier Look to the Princess!

Dedrick Smelling salts for the Princess!

Ola (*stepping forward and giving them to him*) Smelling salts, my lord.

Albern Overcome with love.

Delcine (*coming to*) Oh, God! He is quite appalling!

Albern What is she saying?

Dedrick She says he is a mite enthralling.

Albern So be it! Let us leave the young lovers for a while, that they may –

Delcine Father, wait! (*sotto*) I cannot marry *him*.

Albern (*sotto*) Oh, come, come, come, my daughter . . .

Delcine (*sotto*) It is hard enough to have to marry someone I have never met, but I thought at least I would be marrying a hero. A warrior.

Albern (*sotto*) He is. He is a hero, my dear.

Delcine (*sotto*) But he's – he's so short. And fat.

Albern (*sotto*) Oh, come!

Delcine (*sotto*) And extremely ugly.

Albern (*fiercely*) Enough, child! Any more such talk, I will have you walled up in a dungeon and left to starve to death. You're not too old for that. Unwin is our guest and you will treat him with respect. You will be polite to him, and grant his every wish and, by this evening, see to it you both fall in love. (*louder*) Because tomorrow morning you are to marry him and produce three children within the year, whether you like it or not!

Delcine (*meekly*) Yes, father!

Albern (*mildly again, to the assembly*) We must leave these tender young lovers to sport together, gaily to win each other's heart.

Women (*romantically*) Aaahhhh!

Albern Let us begone!

The court disperses, leaving only Orvin and Delcine. They glare at each other.

Orvin I heard what you said about me, just then.

Delcine Good!

Orvin And may I in turn say this. You may be beautiful, you may be rich but underneath all those fine trimmings, that perfect complexion, that exquisite body – you have all the charm and personality of a dead ferret.

Delcine Oh! My salts! (*She sways, threatening to faint.*)

Orvin And I wouldn't faint in here because I'm not catching you.

Delcine Oh!

She rushes out, passing Varian, Dedrick and Skeets in the doorway.

Varian Delcine! Delcine!

Dedrick We interrupt, sire?

Orvin No.

Dedrick I am Prince Dedrick.

Orvin Indeed? I am Orv – Ulmar. Of course.

Dedrick Of course. My sister appeared distressed.

Orvin Did she? Well . . .

Dedrick I trust there is nothing untoward. (*aside to Varian*) Tush, man! Will you say nothing?

Varian (*glaring at Orvin*) What did you do to her, you coarse, brutish mercenary?

Orvin Eh?

Dedrick (*pushing Varian forward*) Be firm!

Varian You should know that I am Lord Varian and that I am in love with the fair Lady Delcine, who is the most beautiful, most pure, divine creature in the world, and if you lay so much as a grubby little hand upon her, hero or not, I will – (*looking at Dedrick*) – I will challenge you, sire.

Orvin Look, I've no wish to . . .

Varian Good day to you.

Varian strides out.

Dedrick (*going after him*) Varian, my dear fellow . . . (*to Orvin*) I must apologise for Lord Varian. He is somewhat hot-blooded . . . Excuse me.

Dedrick goes off after Varian.

Skeets (*as he follows, smiling nastily*) You would do well, sire, not to offend too many people here. In this castle death may lurk round every corner . . .

Skeets goes off. Orvin is alone.

Orvin (*to the Chorus*) Which is the quickest way out?

Asphodel Get on with it, you fool.

Orvin What?

Griswold Go after her!

Calista Woo her!

Hilliard Win her!

Berengaria You must win the Princess Delcine!

Ingmar It is written in the legend!

Orvin Listen, it is not written in my legend! I can feel it in my bones, this is not going to end well. I am certainly not going to – Ah!

Ola has appeared.

Ola (*nervously*) Oh, My Lord, I crave your pardon. (*looking around, puzzled*) You have someone with you?

Orvin No, no.

Ola I heard voices I – (*shrugging*) My Lord Ulmar, the Princess Delcine apologises for her absence. She has been having a – discussion with her father, the King. She will be here presently.

Orvin I see. And who are you?

Ola My name is Ola, sire, I am the Lady Delcine's maid.

Orvin Ola! That's nice. (*savouring the name*) Ola! Ola! Ola!

Ola (*nervously*) I trust I have not displeased you, sire?

Orvin No. How could you displease me?

Ola I don't know, sire.

Orvin You haven't said anything.

Ola That is seldom a guarantee, sire.

Orvin Please. You may call me Orvin.

Ola I thought your name was Ulmar, sire.

Orvin Yes. It is. But – I am occasionally called Orvin. To my friends.

Ola I could never hope to be included in such company, surely, sire?

Orvin What if I command it?

Ola Sire?

Orvin If I command it. Ola.

Ola (*awkwardly*) Then I would obey, sire. Orwin.

Orvin Orvin.

Ola Orvin.

They stare at each other.

Calista Not that one, you idiot. That is only the maid.

Orvin (*oblivious to this*) Yes, I can – I can see this might end alright, after all.

Ola (*to us*)
Was there ever such a champion as this one?
I have never seen the like in all my days,
He's a funny sort of shape, with little legs, though
I adore it when his eyes are all ablaze.
Given time I think I'd even grow to like him,
Much more than that could never come to pass
For he's a lord and I'm a humble servant,
But, oh, he's got a lovely little –

Delcine is now standing in the doorway.

Delcine Ola!

Ola Oh! My Lady?

Delcine You may leave us, Ola.

Ola My Lady, should I not be here to –

Delcine I said leave us, girl! I feel certain My Lord Ulmar does not pose any serious threat. Certainly not one that I could not deal with. Now go, I say!

Ola (*scuttling out*) My Lady.

Ola goes. Delcine turns to Orvin.

Delcine (*frostily*) So, My Lord. Here I am.

Orvin (*warily*) Yes.

Delcine My father has – persuaded – me to attend you. You may proceed. You have my permission.

Orvin Pardon?

Delcine (*testily*) Is it not customary in your country for a man to press his suit upon the woman he intends to marry?

Orvin – er . . . yes . . .

Delcine To declare his love? To woo her with gentle words?

Orvin Yes. But rarely to a woman who considers him short. Or fat. Or ugly. He draws the line there.

Delcine Consider this. Perchance I am attracted to short, fat, ugly men.

Orvin You are?

Delcine It is possible. If my options are limited, as they are, I would doubtless be attracted to a Barbary ape. Who knows, perhaps you too could in time grow to love a woman with the personality of a dead ferret?

Orvin (*dubious*) It doesn't seem a particularly sound basis for a relationship. Nothing personal.

Delcine Be circumspect, sire. Maybe your own options are also thus limited. More so than you imagine. In my country we have a saying: paupers cannot be pickers.

Orvin Yes, I think we say something similar.

Delcine Then, since I have no wish to be walled up and left to starve to death, I suggest we proceed. I am waiting. Commence your wooing, sire!

Orvin looks about him helplessly.

Chorus
And so it was that Ulmar of Sollistis,
In dulcet tones with winning words,
Did gain the hand of the fair Delcine . . .

The music leads us to the love ballad introduction. Orvin fails lamentably to get the song started.

Orvin
You are – you are the – you are –

– it's very difficult this.

You are – the mmmnnn – of the – mmmnnn –

– if you don't feel it . . .

32

Delcine (*impatiently*) Oh, for heaven's sake, let's get this over with. Very well!

> *Delcine sings the song apparently originally intended for Ulmar to sing to her. She sings it quite sincerely as she obviously believes every word of it. Orvin stands feeling somewhat redundant.*

(*with growing passion and conviction*)
Delcine! Delcine!
Half sweet maiden, half cruel harlot, half a something-
    in-between.
She's a butterfly in motion,
She's bright sunlight on the ocean,
She is timeless, effervescent, evergreen.
Oh sweet Delcine,
One-third angel, one-third devil, one-third child and
    one-third queen,
With her lips full soft and tender,
Whilst her eyes demand surrender,
Her clear skin like Madagascan velveteen.
Such beauty constant and enduring,
All at once elusive yet alluring.
Although cool modesty presumes she,
Such a hunger consumes she –
Delcine! Delcine!
All the wisdom of a woman, still a girl of seventeen,
Her sheer beauty turning other women green,
She's – Delcine! Delcine! Delcine!

> *She finishes in an orgy of self-adoration. Then, brusquely and practically:*

Sire, your honey-sweet words have melted my heart. I am yours!

> *She grabs a startled Orvin and kisses him deeply, but more like someone in need of a drink of water than savouring a wine. Varian, Dedrick and Skeets appear.*

33

Ola following them, from a different direction. Orvin sees them. He and Delcine stop and break apart.

Varian (*coldly*) That, sire, is the woman I love.

Orvin Congratulations.

Varian (*being again pushed forward by Dedrick*) How dare you lay your loutish hands upon her. You have besmirchèd this lady's honour.

Orvin I have not besmirchèd her. I have not touched her. (*to Delcine*) Have I? You tell him.

Dedrick Is this true, Delcine? Did this fellow besmirch you?

Delcine (*hesitantly*) I – er . . .

Dedrick Tell the truth, Delcine.

Delcine Yes. Yes, he besmirchèd me. (*She weeps.*)

Orvin (*indignantly*) I did not.

Delcine I am besmirchèd . . . (*swaying*) My smelling salts! Quickly!

Dedrick (*hurrying to her*) Smelling salts!

Ola (*proffering them*) Smelling salts!

Dedrick Oh, my poor sweet innocent sister!

Dedrick comforts Delcine. She weeps in his arms.

(*crying out dramatically*) Revenge! Revenge! Will no man present avenge my beloved, besmirchèd sister?

Silence.

Dear God! Is there no man here present?

Skeets (*hesitantly*) Well, I will if –

Dedrick (*sotto, sharply*) Not you!

They all look to Varian.

Varian (*he hesitates, looking at them, then*) Yes! Very well. Yes!

Skeets hands Varian a gauntlet he happens to have with him. Varian goes and slaps Orvin in the face with it.

Orvin Ow!

Varian That is for you, sire. (*repeating the gesture*) And that!

Orvin Ow! What are you doing?

Varian Respond, you miserable cur, challenge me! Respond.

Orvin I am responding. Didn't you hear me? I said ow!

Varian Challenge me!

Orvin I'm not challenging anyone. (*to Chorus*) This is turning for the worse, again.

Chorus
And so it was bold Ulmar,
For the sake of love,
Did challenge wretched Varian
In mortal combat to the very death!

Orvin No, he did not.

Varian This lady's honour, sir! I insist it is avenged!

Dedrick Well spoken.

Skeets Well spoken. Well spoken.

Orvin I am not fighting. Alright? I am going home. I'm not fighting anyone.

Varian (*drawing his sword*) You cowardly cur!

Orvin Oh, my God! I'm off!

Orvin runs out. Varian pursues him.

Delcine (*following them*) Varian! Varian! Someone, stop him! If he falls, he could cut himself. Ola!

Ola My Lady!

Delcine goes. Ola follows her.

Skeets It would appear our hero will not fight, My Lord. Curious.

Dedrick Very curious. For a hero. It is usually difficult to prevent them. No matter, we must resort to other means, Skeets.

Skeets What means are these, sire?

Dedrick This evening there is to be a banquet in honour of the bride and groom. Make sure our guest of honour's goblet is well filled. Maybe a little wine will sharpen his temper. Lend our reluctant groom a little fire. Come!

Skeets It will be done, My Lord.

Skeets and Dedrick go off.
  As they do so, Orvin comes on from the other direction, still running, somewhat breathless. A second later, Varian enters in pursuit.

Varian Come here, you lily-livered whey-face!

Orvin runs off. Varian follows.
  Delcine comes on, breathless.

Delcine Varian, my love . . .

Ola comes on behind her.

Try to catch them, Ola.

Ola Yes, My Lady.

Delcine My frail woman's body can run no further. (*as she goes*) I must rest.

Delcine goes back the way she has come.

Ola Yes, My Lady. (*looking about her*) Which way did they . . .?

But Delcine has gone
   Ola is about to go off when Orvin comes running back from another direction.

Orvin Tell me, am I running in a circle?

Ola Yes, sire!

Orvin I thought I was. (*taking off again, as he goes*) And it's Orvin. How many more times? (*Orvin goes out.*)

Ola (*savouring the name*) Orvin . . . Orvin . . . (*She smiles.*)

Varian comes on, still in pursuit of Orvin.

Varian Which way did he go, girl? Did you see?

Ola (*pointing in the opposite direction*) That way, My Lord. Towards the East Tower.

Varian (*triumphantly*) The East Tower? Ha! Then I have him! I have him!

Varian rushes off.

Ola Orvin! (*thoughtfully*)

Given time I think I'd even grow to love him.
If he should ask I'd yield to his request.
I long to feel his manly arms around me,
The touch of his firm lips upon my –

Orvin enters again, still running.

Orvin (*seeing Ola and stopping*) This is hopeless, isn't it? If I run any faster, I'll catch *him* up.

Ola Fear not, he has gone.

Orvin Gone?

Ola To the East Tower.

Orvin The East Tower?

Ola He was – misdirected.

Orvin I see. Thank you. (*looking around*) Who were you talking to just then?

Ola (*also looking round*) No one.

Orvin Might you not get into trouble? When he finds he's been misdirected?

Ola Probably – Orvin.

Orvin Then thank you – Ola.

Silence. They stare at each other.

Ola You need not fear Lord Varian in a fight. He faints at the very sight of blood.

Orvin His own or other people's?

Slight pause. Music under.

Ola Why did you refuse to fight him, Orvin? Truly you are not afraid? Are you not a great warrior?

Orvin (*anxious not to disillusion her*) I'm – it wasn't – the time to fight, you see. There is a time to fight and then there is a time not to fight, you see. We warriors need to know when to judge the occasion. You see?

Ola I see. And how do you judge the – occasion?

Orvin
Now might be the time to mention,
I have not the least intention
Of dying on some distant battlefield.

38

P'rhaps this subject needs an airing,
'Case you think that I'm uncaring,
Behold, my little secret is revealed . . .

I much prefer the living to the dying,
I'm happier to be laughing than be crying,
But if the chips should fall,
Or if your back's against the wall –
The one I'd want to die for would be you.

I much prefer the smiling to the frowning,
I laugh far more when swimming than when drowning,
Although I do declare
If you should ever need me there,
The one I'd surely die for would be you.

Maybe some small explanation –
I've this strong self-preservation,
This tiny warning bell I can't ignore
Tells this sometimes ardent lover,
Time to turn and run for cover
When someone's husband's banging on the door . . .

Ola
I much prefer the flying to the falling,
I'd sooner be embracing than be brawling,
Yet if I hear you call,
I'd take a chance and risk it all,
The one I'd gladly die for would be you.

Both
Perhaps this is the time for clearly stating,
We much prefer the loving to the hating,

Ola
But if the threats grow rife,

Orvin
I will protect you with my life,
The one I'd gladly die for –

Ola

I'd cheat and steal and lie for –

Both

The one I'd want to die for would be you.

The song finishes in an embrace. It is immediately interrupted by the Chorus.

Chorus

And that same evening –!

Orvin (*in mid-kiss*) Hang on, hang on! We're in the middle of a love scene here!

Ola (*startled*) What?

Chorus (*unheeding*)

In honour of the marriage of Ulmar
The Bravest Warrior of Sollistis
To the desirable, most beautiful Princess Delcine
   of Varne –
A glorious celebration!

Celebratory music. The stage is filled with revellers. During this, Orvin is seized by two servants, who lead him off. Ola makes herself scarce, returning later to serve wine and food along with other servants.

   This is the sort of equivalent of a pre-dinner drinks session, with goblets of wine distributed and frequently refilled. Great trays of food are carried through the hall from time to time, from the offstage kitchens en route to the offstage dining room. The feast is frequently applauded and cheered on its way. The Chorus provides merry food-madrigal muzak, under.

Chorus

Bavarois de fromage blanc aux concombres et son
   coulis;
Thon en gelée, aspic d'oefs et mousse de Parme aux
   poireaux;

Paillotes de foie de veaux, ragoût de porc aux coques,
    gaspacho;
Rougets à la provençale, truite à la tomme de
    Savoie;
Noix de Saint-Jacques au jambon et crème chantilly
    Nata;
Bon appetit, bon appetit, bon appetit et merci . . .

*Amongst the crowd is Varian, who seems far from
happy. Dedrick and Skeets also lurk on the fringes,
waiting.*
    *As the madrigal ends, a fanfare as Orvin returns.
He has been decked out in some rather splendid
finery.*
    A great cheer greets his arrival.

Chorus
    All hail the hero Ulmar!
    The mighty warrior from Sollistis!

Diners (*raising their goblets*)
    All hail the hero Ulmar!
    The mighty warrior from Sollistis!

*Orvin acknowledges this with a suitably modest wave.
Another fanfare. This time it heralds the arrival of
Albern. On his arm is Delcine, decked out in all her
glory and looking lovelier than ever.*

Chorus
    All hail with good King Albern,
    His lovely daughter Princess Delcine!

Diners (*raising their goblets*)
    All hail with good King Albern,
    His lovely daughter Princess Delcine!

Attendant Pray silence for His Majesty!

Everything stops.

Albern Dear friends and loyal subjects! This banquet is, of course, in honour of the forthcoming union between the noble – the noble – warrior – Irma –

Dedrick (*sotto*) Ulmar . . .

Albern – Ongar – and my most precious daughter, Delcine . . . Tonight is a night for celebration, friends, for feasting, for drinking, for making merry. But first let there be dancing! I –

Dedrick Father!

Albern What is it now, Dedrick? You're always interrupting, boy!

Dedrick Excuse me, father, but is it not customary for the groom first to toast his bride to be?

Albern Toast his –? Oh, good idea! Of course. First I call upon – er –

Dedrick (*rapidly*) – the valiant warrior Ulmar to toast his lovely bride!

Albern – lovely bride, yes.

> *Dedrick signals to Skeets, who now steps forward with an enormous goblet of wine. It contains several bottles.*

Orvin (*taking the goblet with some alarm*) All of it?

Skeets (*sotto*) Tradition demands it. Say after me,

I drink this wine –

Orvin
I drink this wine –

Skeets (*sotto*)
– to the very last drop –

Orvin
– to the very last drop –

Skeets (*sotto*)
– to signify my love and undying devotion –

Orvin
– to signify my love and undying devotion –

Skeets (*sotto*) –
– for the most beautiful and radiant of brides-to-be!

Orvin
– for the most beautiful and radiant of brides-to-be!

He hesitates.

Skeets (*sotto*) Go on then, drink it!

All (*chanting*) Drink! Drink! Drink! Drink! Drink!

Orvin drains the goblet. It takes a little time.

(*as he drinks*) Whheeeyyyyyyyyyyyyyyyyyy!

Applause as he finishes. He is now well on the way to being very drunk indeed.

Attendant Your attention for the Lord Ulmar and the lovely Princess Delcine, who will now lead the dance.

The dance music starts up. As everyone draws back to the edges of the room, Orvin finds himself alone on the floor with Delcine. He stands helplessly. He smiles rather vacantly.

Delcine (*sotto*) Come on, you fat fool. Do not tell me you cannot dance either?

Orvin Only – only a sort of jig.

Delcine (*holding out her hand, sotto*) Well, we had better make the best of it, had we not? (*louder*) Come, My Lord, everyone desires to follow us.

The dance starts. It is obviously the intention that, whatever Delcine and Orvin do, the rest try to follow.

In the case of Delcine and Orvin this is very difficult, since their steps, thanks to Orvin, are far from conventional.

(*as they dance*) Ow! . . . Ah . . . Ow . . . Be careful, you fool! Ow! (*etc.*)

Orvin (*as they dance*) Sorry! Sorry . . . I'm so sorry . . . sorry . . . (*etc.*)

Dancers (*variously*) Ow! Ooo! Ow! Sorry . . . so sorry . . . (*etc.*)

The dance finally ends with a bow and a curtsey and a great deal of banging of heads.

Orvin (*very drunk*) Thank you very much.

Delcine (*moving away from Orvin*) You clumsy oaf. I'd sooner marry a baboon!

Orvin Mutual! You ff–erret.

Servant If it so please Your Majesties, dinner is served!

Led off by Albern and Delcine, the room rapidly empties as the guests all go into dinner.
Only Orvin is left, looking slightly dazed.

Orvin (*staggering slightly*) Which way's the food?

Varian re-enters.

(*seeing him*) Oh, no!

Varian You are aware, are you not, that you have just made the Princess Delcine a laughing stock?

Orvin It isn't my fault if she can't dance . . .

Varian (*yelling*) You are a barbarian and a bumpkin. Do you hear me?

Orvin I can't help hearing you, you're – deafening . . .

Varian Have you nothing to say to me? Nothing at all? Are you such a cringing pathetic coward?

Orvin Yes, alright. I've got something to say to you. I've got something to say to you. You want my opinion of you? You want to hear my opinion of you?

Varian I welcome your reply, sire.

Orvin (*beginning to speak with difficulty*) Very well. You are a stuck-up, conceited, loud-mouthed, useless, unattractive, ignorant, upper-class, chinless twit!

   Pause.

Varian What did you call me?

   Pause. Orvin reflects.

Orvin I can't remember now. Oh, yes, a stuck-up, conceited, loud-mouthed, use – Stand still . . . Stand still while I'm talking to . . . (*apparently seeing two Varians*) Who's your friend?

   He collapses and falls to the ground unconscious.

Varian (*outraged*) Get up! Get up and repeat that, do you hear me? Get up, at once!

   But Orvin is dead to the world.
   Dedrick and Skeets, who can't have been far away, enter.

Dedrick What has happened?

Varian The man has fainted! He refused to fight, called me – hurtful things – and then fainted.

Dedrick Did he now?

Skeets You were not reciting your poetry to him, by any chance?

Varian (*angrily*) No, I was not! What are we going to do? He refuses to fight? What can you do with a man who refuses to –

Ola has entered from the dining room. She has also been watching, we suspect.

Dedrick (*seeing Ola, to Varian*) Sshh! (*to Ola*) You, girl! Help this man to his room!

Ola Me, sire?

Dedrick Yes, you sire.

Ola Yes, sire.

Dedrick (*close to her, smiling nastily*) Such pretty eyes.

Ola moves with alacrity, alarmed by his expression. She shakes Orvin awake.

Ola Come along! Come along, My Lord . . . Come! Come with me!

Orvin (*groggily*) Whatsa – where – er – who-wa-you . . . wa-wa . . . Oh, hello.

Ola helps Orvin to his feet. He staggers. She supports him.

Ola That's it! That's it! This way.

Orvin (*as they go*) Wa . . . wa-wa . . . wa . . .

Ola, half-supporting him, leads Orvin off. The others stand watching.

Varian (*once they have gone*) What are we to do?

Dedrick I fear we must resort, My Lord, to an alternative plan. It appears that the man is reluctant, nay I would go so far as to say incapable of fighting, so we must employ other means.

Varian Other means? What other –?

Dedrick Rather more crude, I fear, but equally effective. In short, My Lord Varian, you will wait until the man is asleep, which should be in all of two minutes after he reaches his bed. You will then enter his bedchamber and slit his throat whilst he sleeps.

Varian (*taken aback*) I will do what? Slit his –?

Dedrick You still wish to marry my sister?

Varian Yes, but I feel that – I mean –

Dedrick You have some alternative plan of your own, perhaps –?

Varian (*flustered*) No, no, I do not but –

Dedrick May I remind you that if Ulmar should awaken tomorrow morning, then by noon he will be Delcine's husband. Is that your wish?

Varian No, but –

Dedrick It is not your wish?

Varian Of course not.

 Dedrick produces a dagger.

Dedrick Then do it, My Lord. Do it.

Varian (*after a slight hesitation*) Very well. (*He takes the dagger.*) For Delcine!

Dedrick (*gripping Varian's arm*) A true hero!

 Varian makes to go off after Orvin and Ola.

Varian! Wait a few moments, till he's sound asleep, will you not?

Varian I will.

 Varian goes.

Skeets You think he'll do it? You think he has the stomach?

Dedrick (*shrugging*) Who can tell what a feeble mind will do, given a strong motive? Go with him, Skeets. Follow him. The Lord Varian may need – moral support.

Skeets Support?

Dedrick We also need to witness what he has done. I would hate for such a cowardly act to go unpunished. Make sure you are witness to it, Skeets.

Skeets (*smiling*) Aye, My Lord.

Skeets goes off. Dedrick smiles to himself. The intro has started for Dedrick's song.

Dedrick
  Since I was a child, I have dreamt of the day –

The Chorus thunder in over the top of him, drowning him out as a big bed is brought on.

Chorus
  Meanwhile –

Dedrick (*frustratedly*) Oh confound it! Later!

Dedrick goes off.

Chorus
  – in the bedchamber –
  Of Ulmar mighty warrior –

Orvin, supported by Ola, is assisted to the bed.

Ola (*slightly breathless*) This way, that's it! There!

Orvin (*collapsing*) Wa!

Ola Do you want me to –? Should I help you to –? I'll take your boots off, shall I?

Orvin That would be very kind. I can't reach my feet. They're too far away. Thank you.

Ola (*as she struggles*) Why – why did you drink so much?

Orvin I didn't. I only had the one goblet . . . That's all I had.

Ola It contained at least five flagons.

Orvin Did it really?

Ola It must have done.

She succeeds in getting his boots off.

There! They were trying to get you drunk. I saw them. Would you like me to –? Shall I help you to take off your coat?

Orvin That would be very kind. I don't think I can get my arms that far.

Ola Here. Let me.

They struggle. It is a difficult manoeuvre, given Orvin's condition.

Orvin You have the most beautiful eyes I have ever seen . . .

Ola Thank you. Pull . . .

Orvin As for your lips . . .

Ola (*struggling*) Please, Orvin, try to help a little . . .

Orvin They are the most perfectly formed – delicious shape – your lips . . .

Ola Orvin! Come along.

Orvin As for your nose – I adore your nose – Ola – Ola – The sum of your parts makes you the most beautiful woman I have ever seen in my life . . .

Ola That is the wine talking, Orvin.

Orvin No, no, no. In very vinas. In venus very very. It is me, Orvin, talking. I can hear me. Ola. I love you, Ola.

Ola Please, Orvin. This is not the time. If someone were to find me here –

Orvin If someone found you here, and tried to harm a little hair of your little head. A single little lovely soft hair on your little hairy head. I would fight them for you, Ola. Fear not.

(*drowsily*) Perhaps this is the time for clearly stating,
I much prefer the loving to the hating,

Ola cradles him in her arms.

Both
But if the threats grow rife,
I will protect you with my life,
The one I'd gladly die for –
I'd cheat and steal and lie for –

Orvin has fallen asleep.

Ola (*softly*)
The one I'd want to die for would be you.

Ola curls up on the bed beside Orvin. The two of them lie entwined.
   In a moment, Varian comes on with the dagger. He stops and stares in amazement. Skeets comes in behind him.

Varian (*softly*) What is he doing? What is he doing now? (*loudly*) Stop that! Stop that, do you hear, you animal? (*He kicks the bed.*)

Orvin (*waking*) Ah!

Ola Oh!

Varian, still brandishing the knife, lunges at the pair, beside himself with fury.

Varian You lecherous swine! Not content with defiling my beloved, you now start on the servants!

Ola screams.

Orvin (*alarmed*) Hey! Hey! Hey! Hey!

Skeets (*mildly*) My Lord, calmly! Calmly, My Lord.

Varian (*chasing them round the bed*) I'm going to – to feed you to the swans . . .

Ola screams again.

Orvin What's the matter with the man? Call him off! Call him off!

Skeets (*ineffectually*) My Lord, you must control yourself . . . My Lord!

Dedrick enters during this commotion.

Dedrick (*with great authority*) Stop! Stop at once, I say!

They all stop.

What is this commotion? Explain this brouhaha!

Orvin This man – burst in here –

Ola With a knife –

Varian They were both – in the – on the bed –

Dedrick In the bed?

Varian On the bed. Both of them.

Dedrick Is this true?

Skeets True, My Lord. I just occasioned to be passing and I –

Dedrick You, My Lord Ulmar, and this – girl? This trollop?

Orvin Kindly do not refer to this lady as a trollop.

Dedrick No? What else do you suggest I call her, pray?

Orvin This – is my – betrothèd.

Ola (*faintly*) I am?

Dedrick Betrothèd, indeed? This morrow you are to marry my sister. Had you forgotten? Perhaps it had escaped your mind?

Orvin I don't want to marry your sister.

Dedrick Indeed? You have an explanation for that?

Orvin I have two. She doesn't like me and I don't like her. Good enough?

Delcine enters hurriedly.

Delcine What is happening, brother? I heard the – (*seeing the others*) Oh!

Dedrick Please wait outside, my dear.

Delcine What is happening? Why are they –?

Dedrick Skeets, look to my sister. This is not for your eyes, my sweet.

Skeets (*taking Delcine's arm*) This way, My Lady . . .

Skeets tries to steer Delcine gently but firmly from the room. Delcine resists.

Delcine No! Brother, I wish to know what occurs here. Tell me what is happening? Please.

Varian (*assisting Skeets*) Come, beloved, come with us.

Delcine is reluctantly dragged away by the two men. Dedrick remains.

Dedrick You have insulted my sister in her own castle, sire. And in insulting her, you have insulted our family, including myself. You will fight me, sire, tomorrow at dawn. And I swear one of us will die. Goodnight to you. As for you – mistress – I would feast upon those lovely eyes this night, sire. For tomorrow they will be swollen red with rivers of tears. Till dawn.

Dedrick goes.

Ola (*in a little voice*) What shall we do?

Orvin Fear not.

Ola What?

Orvin Fear not.

Pause.

What am I saying? I'm terrified!

Music.
Blackout.

End of Act One.

Act Two

Blackout.

The armed figures from the Zeva town clock appear as before and strike seven.

In the darkness the Chorus then sets the scene for the second half.

Chorus (*softly at first*)
And so it was that Ulmar,
Great champion of Sollistis,
Enjoyed untroubled sleep,
Filled with the sweetest dreams of Princess Delcine.
But, when the cock crowed, then did this bold warrior
Spring from his bed with a mighty roar of:
(*very loud*) VENGEANCE!

The lights come up suddenly with this last word, bright and sunny. We are still in Orvin's bedroom. He sits up in bed, shocked awake by the sound and bright light. He is very hung-over.

Orvin (*shattered*) Oh, my God! (*He touches his head, gingerly.*)

Chorus (*brightly, continuing*)
Then did bold Ulmar awake, and prepared
For the morning conflict, did buckle on his trusty
    sword,
And put on his –

Orvin Excuse me! Oy!

The Chorus stops.

Sorry to interrupt. Are you sure he does all this?

Flavia It is written . . .

Kenrick . . . in the legend . . .

Calista . . . the legend of Ulmar!

Orvin Yes. Fine. But doesn't this legend say anything about him having breakfast first?

Berengaria Breakfast?

Hilliard Breakfast?

Disa No hero has ever put off battle for breakfast . . .

Orvin Well, you'll pardon me for pointing this out, but as my old mother would say, how on earth will he get through the day without his breakfast?

Elva Breakfast?

Chorus Breakfast.

> And so it was that Ulmar,
> Great champion of Sollistis –

Orvin I say, excuse me . . .

The Chorus stop.

Could you keep it down, just a fraction, please. It's my head, you see . . .

Chorus (*softer*)
> – great champion of Sollistis –
> Enjoyed untroubled sleep,
> Filled with the sweetest dreams of Princess Delcine.
> But, when the cock crowed, then did this bold warrior
> Spring from his bed with a mighty roar of:
> (*very loud*) BREAKFAST!

Orvin jumps at the sudden increase in volume.
Simultaneously Ola enters with a large tray of breakfast.

Ola Good morrow – (*with a smile*) – Orvin . . .

Orvin Ah, that's a welcome sight!

Ola (*thinking he means her, modestly*) Thank you. Did you sleep soundly? (*Ola places the tray on the bed.*)

Orvin Yes, I believe I did, yes. Did you?

Ola Eventually. It was a night to remember.

Orvin It was. (*remembering nothing*) Was it?

Ola I shall never forget it, Orvin.

Orvin Nor will I.

Ola You do remember?

Orvin Oh, yes . . . every second . . .

Ola How you first took my . . .?

Orvin How could I forget?

Ola And then held me in your . . .?

Orvin Oh, yes . . .

Ola Before putting your . . .?

Orvin How could I ever forget that? (*to himself*) My God, what have I missed? (*turning to the breakfast*) Right, let's get started on this, then.

Ola Orvin, my love, you have no time for eating –

Orvin What?

Ola The breakfast was but a ruse to allow me in here without arousing suspicion. My Lady Delcine wishes to see you in her chambers.

Orvin Me? What does she want to see me for?

Ola She will explain.

Orvin The last time we met she called me a baboon.

Ola Please, be quick. She is anxious that her brother's spies do not learn of this meeting. I am to lead you through the secret passage.

Orvin Right. Secret passage. (*surveying the tray*) Can't I even have –?

Ola (*taking his hand*) Please, there is very little time. The duel is due to start within the hour.

Ola presses on the panelling in the wall. It is very probably non-existent.

Orvin What are you doing?

Ola I am pressing on this beautifully carved mediaeval oak panelling, looking for the concealed catch that will open the door to the secret passage. (*She finds the catch.*) Ah! There! Follow me.

Orvin Marvellous!

Chorus
And thus did Ola, the maid, lead Ulmar, the warrior –

Orvin (*to Chorus*) Shh! This is a secret passage!

The Chorus sing softly and wordlessly under the next.

Ola (*to Orvin*) Sssh! Quietly! Who were you talking to?

Orvin No matter. (*as they go along*) It was good, you say, last night, was it? For you?

Ola You were a true champion.

Orvin That's nice. I've never been called that before . . . (*He smiles.*)

Asphodel She's having you on, you fool . . .

Orvin What?

Ola What?

Berengaria You fell asleep on her. Immediately.

Calista Like a dead weight. And snored!

Disa It took her an hour to wriggle out from under you . . .

Elva . . . and get back to the comfort of her own bed.

Flavia So you can wipe that stupid smile off your face.

Women Typical!

Orvin (*a bit crestfallen*) Ah, well. (*defiant*) Who cares? I love her.

Ola (*stopping*) You love who?

Orvin Er – you.

Ola Me?

Orvin Yes.

Ola Love?

Orvin Yes.

Ola I see. I love you, too.

Orvin Ah . . .

> *They stare at each other again. Music.*

Orvin You're so beautiful. (*to the Chorus*) She's so beautiful.

Kenrick She's the wrong one!

Orvin Who cares? Who cares?

> *Ola is in a dream of her own.*

Ola
I recall last night when I undressed him
He lay there looking vulnerable and young,

I longed to lie beside him for a moment,
Explore his naked body with my –

*Delcine appears and opens the secret panel. Light
floods in upon Orvin and Ola.*

Delcine What are you doing?

Orvin Ah!

Ola Oh! My Lady, I –

Delcine Come out of that secret passage, at once. Both
of you!

*Ola and Orvin emerge from the secret passage. They
are in Delcine's bedchamber. The bed has moved, the
tray has gone.*

We have little time. (*calling*) It is them, you can come
out!

Varian comes out from under the bed.

Orvin (*backing away warily*) Oh, no. Not him!

Delcine Wait! Wait! Time is scarce. Listen. Things have
changed. I have learnt through my spies that my brother
Dedrick not only plans to kill you, Ulmar – but also my
beloved Varian . . .

Varian I knew we could never trust him!

Delcine What are you saying? You trusted him every
inch of the way, Varian. That is why we are in this
predicament. What is more there are signs that, having
once disposed of Varian, he plots a similar fate for me.
Me! His own sister!

Orvin Fie!

Delcine We have therefore worked out a plan, Varian
and I.

Orvin A plan?

Delcine It is simple. When you fight Dedrick, you must kill him before he kills you.

Orvin With a sword?

Varian Of course with a sword.

Orvin There is a small problem.

Delcine What is that?

Orvin I have never used a sword before in my life.

Varian Never –?

Orvin Except for chopping wood. And I got a whipping for that.

Delcine What sort of warrior are you, pray?

Orvin I am no sort of warrior. (*indicating Varian*) Why doesn't he fight him? He's always looking for a fight.

Delcine (*protectively*) Varian – is not able to fight, he . . . He – he . . .

Varian I faint at the sight of blood. Go on, say it!

Delcine He faints at the sight of blood.

Orvin Oh, yes he faints at the sight of blood, of course.

Ola He faints at the sight of blood . . .

Varian Alright! Alright, everybody say it!

Chorus
He faints at the sight of blood!

Delcine No, it cannot be Varian, it has to be you, Ulmar. Do not fear, we have taken – precautions. The sword you will be given has a powerful poison at its tip. You have only to inflict a scratch upon Dedrick and he will be dead within seconds.

Orvin How do you propose I scratch him? Wait till he falls asleep? (*coming to a decision*) Listen, I have to tell you. I am not Ulmar. I'm sorry. But I am not him. He. (*looking at Ola*) I'm sorry.

Ola You're not –?

Orvin No.

Delcine What are you saying? Who are you, if not Ulmar?

Orvin I'm – Orvin.

Ola Only to your special friends?

Orvin No, I'm Orvin to everyone as well. I am – I was Lord Ulmar's squire. I – accidentally – allowed him to become – killed . . .

Varian You allowed him to –?

Delcine Killed?

Ola Orvin?

Orvin I'm sorry. I am not a hero. I am nobody. (*looking at Ola again*) A nobody. I'm sorry.

> Silence. The three stare at him. They freeze. Suspended chord under.

What's happening? What's happened to them?

Griswold You may well ask.

Asphodel We have been forced to stop time, Orvin.

Hilliard To pause in our narrative.

Berengaria Which you should know is unheard of!

Orvin What else do you suggest I do? What else can I do but tell the truth?

Ingmar What truth?

Orvin This truth. My truth.

Calista *Your* truth? What is your truth?

Orvin My truth? My truth is – that I'm an ordinary bloke. I'm a squire. I'm not a hero. My name isn't Ulmar, it's Orvin. I'm scared, I can't fight. (*pointing at Varian*) I don't like him at all. (*pointing at Delcine*) I'm not too keen on her, (*pointing at Ola*) and I'm in love with this one. That's my truth. Right.

Junius Quite immaterial . . .

Orvin Maybe – to you it is . . . But we're human beings here, you know. Most of us.

Disa (*gently*) Orvin. You are now part of a legend. A legend that needs to be told. You cannot turn back.

Orvin But what if I –?

Elva You cannot turn back, Orvin. It is written.

Kenrick The only truth is to continue the legend.

Orvin Don't I even get an appeal?

Lathrop It is the only way . . .

Orvin What about her? What about Ola?

Flavia Continue!

Orvin If anything happens to her . . .

Griswold Continue!

Orvin Not until I have your promise.

Hilliard Promise? What promise?

Orvin That – whatever happens to me – she will be safe. Ola will not be harmed. I want your promise on that.

Asphodel Our promise?

Ingmar Gods don't make promises.

Berengaria Not to mere mortals.

Orvin Then I'm not going on. (*sitting on the ground*) I refuse to carry on.

Junius She's not even a princess . . .

Calista She's a maid.

Orvin Those are my terms. Take 'em or leave 'em.

Kenrick Oh – very well.

Disa Very well.

Orvin I have your promise? She'll be alright. She'll be safe?

Lathrop She'll be safe.

Orvin You promise?

Chorus We promise!

Elva Now can we get on with it, please?

Orvin (*rising*) Right! On we go, then!

Chorus
And so it came about that Ulmar,
Bold champion and warrior of Sollistis –
To protect the beautiful Princess Delcine
Agreed to fight the evil Dedrick
With the poisoned sword.

Delcine (*hugging Orvin*) Oh, thank you! Brave, brave Ulmar!

Varian (*shaking his hand*) Thank you!

Delcine My bold champion!

Ola (*smiling at Orvin*) My hero!

Orvin (*half to himself*) This is never going to work.

Varian For the duel you will need a second. I would do it myself, only I fear –

Orvin – that when he runs me through, you'll faint. We can't have that!

Delcine No, we cannot. If Varian were to fall and harm himself . . . We will find you someone less valuable and more reliable.

Orvin Am I allowed to choose for myself?

Varian Of course.

Orvin (*pointing at Ola*) Then I choose her.

Ola Me?

Varian Her?

Delcine You cannot choose her.

Orvin Why not?

Delcine She's a – she's a girl.

Orvin So? You have something against girls?

Delcine No. Only –

Orvin (*to Ola*) Tell me, do you faint at the sight of blood?

Ola No.

Orvin And when I'm lying there dying, will you solemnly promise to give me a final lingering kiss?

Ola I promise.

Orvin I choose her.

Delcine Oh, very well. It is not – proper! Come! I will give you the sword. It has been prepared. Follow me!

Varian Follow on!

Delcine and Varian leave.

Ola (*as they are about to follow*) One thing –

Orvin What?

Ola You will not die, Orvin. Do you hear me?

Orvin Are you sure of that?

Ola (*fiercely*) A man like you enters a life such as mine but once in a lifetime. If at all. And I refuse to lose you now. Come!

Ola leaves.

Orvin (*as he follows her*) The world is filled with strong women . . .

Orvin goes. Under the next the bed is struck as Dedrick and Skeets enter. A wooden throne is brought on, plus a table and chair.

Dedrick (*conspiratorially*) You have done everything that I asked?

Skeets Aye, My Lord.

Dedrick
You've planned things for my sister's final journey to
   her maker?

Skeets
Well, her journey only takes her to the local
   undertaker –
But it's hardly my affair
Where she travels to from there –
Who can tell and who could care?

Dedrick
You've carried out my wishes and instructions to the
letter?

Skeets
I can safely guarantee that no one else could do it
better.
Ev'ry detail has been planned,
I have woven ev'ry strand,
And I have it all in hand.

Dedrick
You have my solemn promise at my future coronation,
I'll reward your loyal service with some social elevation,
There's no telling that you might,
Kneel one day and rise a knight,
If you make this all come right . . .

Skeets shows Dedrick the throne.

Skeets
Behold the chair where sits our noble King,
And now observe the knife, the hidden spring . . .

*Skeets operates a mechanism at the back of the chair.
There is a 'clunk' and a concealed knife springs out
of the back of the chair. Anyone sitting in it would be
instantly impaled.*

The King is dead, alas –

Dedrick (*smiling*)
Long live the King!

*Dedrick grips Skeets's hand and leaves swiftly. Skeets
reloads the knife mechanism.*

Skeets
In ten long years,
I've grown to know him,
I wouldn't trust the man as far as I could throw him.

Nonetheless, you understand,
I have everything in hand.

Delcine enters cautiously.

Delcine

Hail! Loyal friend and subject, you have done what
  I requested?

Skeets produces a small vial of poison from his pocket.

Skeets

My Lady, here's a poison that I've previously tested . . .
He need only take a sip,
Just a solitary drip,
A mere droplet on his lip.
Just dissolve it in the goblet and it matters not who
  loses,
This will then dispatch the winner and the one that
  fortune chooses.
Be it Ulmar who lies dead,
Or Lord Dedrick's killed instead.

Delcine

I will do just as you've said.
(*fiercely*) How strong my courage and how unafraid,
How fiercely anger doth my blood pervade,
God help the man whose sister he's betrayed.

*She puts a bag of money into Skeets's hand and goes
off, swiftly, clutching the vial of poison.*

Skeets

Be she a wife,
A sister, jilted bride,
It pays to have the woman on your side.
Never build a house on sand.
I have everything in hand.

A fanfare. Skeets moves away to a corner instantly.

Chorus

And so they came,
The noble King Albern and fair Delcine –

Delcine enters on the arm of Albern. She carries an ornate silver goblet filled with wine. She places the goblet on the table and sits beside it in her own chair. Albern moves to the throne and remains standing whilst the others enter. He seems even frailer than before.

To watch the greatest contest
That the world had ever known –
First came the evil Dedrick –

Dedrick enters in black. Ready for battle.
Skeets takes his place near Dedrick, evidently his second.

Women Aaaaaah!

Chorus

And last there came like
Heracles!
Like Magog, Gog, like Antaeus,
Like Ulysses!
There entered through the door,
Great Ulmar, mightiest champion of Sollistis.

Orvin enters, trying to live up to the introduction. He is followed by Ola.

Courtier Pray silence for His Majesty!

Albern Tell first the reason for this mortal combat.

Courtier Your Majesty, it is alleged by Prince Dedrick that Ulmar of Sollistis did impugn the honour of the fair Princess Delcine –

Albern Impugn?

Courtier Sire. And did further besmirch her and defile her in a manner unbefitting to a hero.

Albern Besmirch?

Courtier Sire.

Albern Is this true, daughter? You have been besmirchèd?

Delcine (*meekly*) Yes, father.

Albern Dear oh dear. (*to Orvin*) Do you admit this charge?

Orvin No, I don't!

Albern Do you know that the penalty for besmirchment in this realm is quick and sudden death?

Orvin No, I didn't. But I'm not at all surprised.

Albern And that is just for besmirching a commoner. An ordinary run-of-the-mill woman. We are speaking of my daughter, here. A royal princess. What do you suppose the penalty for that should be?

Orvin No idea. Strangled at birth?

Dedrick Father, I pray you let the duel commence. I long to avenge my most dear sister's honour.

Albern Very well, let it commence. And may the best man win. (*glaring at Orvin*) But not you.

Courtier Take up your swords!

> *Orvin is handed a sword by Ola. She looks at the sword significantly. Orvin handles it with care.*
> *Meanwhile, Dedrick likewise has his sword handed to him by Skeets.*

Courtier Prepare!

Dedrick (*with an elaborate flourish*) I salute you, sire!

Orvin (*suspiciously*) Oh, yes?

Dedrick And I thank merciful God that He has chosen me as the instrument of your death.

Orvin We'll see.

Courtier Commence!

Dedrick comes at Orvin, blade whirling. He's an impressive swordsman. It is only the fact that Orvin is so unconventional that somewhat throws Dedrick off balance. This probably saves Orvin from being killed in the first five seconds. The Chorus, though, appear oblivious to what is happening, preferring to sing their own 'official' version of events.

Chorus
Then came brave Ulmar, that greatest of champions,
Whirling his sword with the guile of a warrior,

Orvin (*taking furious evasive action*) You sure about that?

Chorus
Seasoned in battle and heedless of jeopardy,
Fearlessly forward to challenge the evil Prince
Dedrick, pretender and ruthless conspirator,
Put now to flight by the blade of the mighty one.
Ulmar! Brave Ulmar! With one voice the people cried!

Orvin swishes at Dedrick but instead hits Skeets in the leg. The Chorus continue oblivious.

See how the forces of darkness are vanquishèd,
Witness false Dedrick, now trembling and terrified –

Skeets (*over this last, clutching his leg*) Ahh!

Orvin (*continuing to avoid Dedrick*) Sorry.

As the fight continues, Skeets draws his hand from his leg. It is covered in blood. He staggers in the direction of Varian.

Skeets Ah! Ah! My leg! My leg! It burns.

Varian Sirrah, are you injured?

Courtier Put up your swords!

Dedrick and Orvin stop fighting momentarily. The Chorus stops.

Look to the gentleman!

Skeets (*holding out his hand to Varian*) I'm dying. Help, help me, I'm dying.

Varian (*at the sight of the blood*) Oh dear, God . . . (*He sways and starts to faint.*)

Delcine (*alarmed*) Varian! My sweet!

Courtier Look to Lord Varian!

Varian is helped to Delcine's chair.

Delcine Smelling salts, quickly. (*to Ola*) Quickly, girl. You have some there?

Ola (*finding them*) These are fresh today, My Lady. (*She gives the salts to Delcine.*)

Skeets (*weakly, he is fading fast*) No! Not – the – salts – not – the – smelling – salts . . .

Delcine What does he say?

Ola Here, My Lady!

Skeets (*feebly extending an arm*) No . . . .

Skeets dies.

Archbishop (*examining Skeets*) This man is dead! May his soul rest in peace!

Courtier Have at! Lay on!

Orvin and Dedrick resume. So do the Chorus.

Chorus
    Kneeling before this bold winner and conqueror –
    Thus was it written, this legend of victory,
    Down through the centuries, of Ulmar the mighty one!

    During this:

Delcine (*administering the salts to Varian*) Here, my love, here! Breathe deeply!

    Varian's head jerks back.

Varian (*in shock, going rigid*) Mmmmmeeeearrr!

Delcine What is it? What is it?

Ola (*comprehending*) My Lady! The salts! Don't touch them! They are poisoned!

Delcine What?

Courtier Put up your swords!

    Dedrick and Orvin stop fighting momentarily. The Chorus stop again.

    Look to Lord Varian!

Delcine (*to Ola*) Is this your doing, girl?

Ola No, My Lady, it was . . . (*She looks at the body of Skeets.*)

Delcine (*glaring at Skeets*) Treachery!

Varian (*gasping for breath*) Delcine!

Delcine Oh, my darling!

Varian I am dying!

Delcine (*wailing*) No, no, no! (*She clasps Varian to her.*)

Albern (*irritably*) Enough! Cease that infernal wailing and on with the fight, I say!

Courtier Have at! Lay on!

Orvin and Dedrick resume. So do the Chorus.

Chorus
Let it be sung whilst mankind has a memory,
Be it related in castles and villages –

During this:

Delcine Oh, Varian!

Varian My darling! (*singing weakly*) When . . . when . . .

Delcine Stop! Stop! He is trying to say something . . .

Courtier Put up your swords!

Dedrick and Orvin stop fighting. The Chorus stop again.

Varian (*weakly*)
When in the graveyard we are quietly resting . . .

Delcine starts to sway uncertainly.

Delcine (*feeling dizzy*) Oh . . .

Courtier Look to the lady!

Varian
People will recall those dying words that we both said
Upon our last and final breath
Till death! Sweet dea-t-t-t-h-h-h . . .

Varian dies, still in the chair.

Delcine He's dead. My beloved Varian is dead!

Albern Then on with the fight!

Courtier Have at! Lay on!

Orvin and Dedrick resume. So do the Chorus

Chorus
> There in the church, every schoolroom and market
>   place,
> Round the night fire let the parents retell of it,
> Bidding their children to heed and remember it,
> This is the day when all Darkness was banishèd!

During this, Ola supports Delcine.

Ola A chair for My Lady.

Albern Oh, for heaven's sake sit here!

Albern gets up irritably to allow Ola to sit Delcine down on the throne. He keeps his eyes fixed on the battle. He moves round the back of the throne to watch.
Orvin finally loses his sword. He lies helpless as Dedrick stands over him.
The Chorus finish their narration.

Dedrick (*looking to Albern*) Thus is my precious sister avenged! Which is it, father? Mercy or – death?

Albern (*thumping the back of the throne with his fist*) Death, son! Death!

There is a clunk and Delcine goes rigid, her eyes wide open in shock. No one appears to notice.

Dedrick So be it. Death it shall be!

He kicks Orvin's sword some distance away from him. He then swaggers to the table, takes up the goblet and toasts Delcine.

My divine, most pure sister! The victor salutes you!

He swigs the contents in one and returns to Orvin.

(*softly*) And now – you besmircher of womankind – prepare to die like a dog . . .

Ola (*averting her eyes, softly*) Oh, no . . . Please . . .

Orvin (*to Chorus*) This is not the ending I had in mind.

A freeze.

Griswold How do you mean?

Asphodel We kept our promise.

Orvin What promise? What about her? What about Ola?

Hilliard What about her?

Berengaria She's safe.

Ingmar She's perfectly happy.

Orvin Happy? *Happy?* Look at her. Just look at her!

Ola stands in frozen misery, her hands clasped in prayer.

Calista (*romantically*) Ah!

Disa I think she's praying, isn't she?

Junius Praying? Who on earth is she praying to, do you think?

Elva Us, presumably.

Kenrick Us?

Flavia Fat chance!

Griswold Onwards!

Chorus Onwards!

Orvin makes himself as small as possible. His eyes also closed.

Dedrick (*resuming, softly*) And now – you besmircher of womankind – prepare to die like a dog . . . (*He begins to feel a little dizzy and stands uncertainly.*)

Ola
Does it end like this, my love, our story?
This slender volume, pages yet not writ,
No more, my sweet, no more, the final chapter.
Oh, cruel world! Oh death! Oh Lord! Oh –!

Albern (*finally losing patience, interrupting Ola*) Come
on, my son! Do it now! Dispatch him!

*Instead, Dedrick convulses slightly as the poison takes
hold. He staggers, seeming to have trouble focusing
on the prostrate Orvin. He drops his sword.*

Dedrick (*in amazement*) I have been poisoned. *I* am
poisoned! *I*? Who has done this –? (*He stares at Delcine,
in disbelief.*) My sister? My beloved – sister? (*realising*)
You – bitch from hell! (*He drops to his knees.*)

Courtier Look to the Prince!

Dedrick Wait! Wait! I have something to say . . .

(*weakly at first*) Since I was a child, I have dreamt of
the day . . .
I would stand here the master of all I survey.
As a youth I was not like conventional boys
With their games, cruel names and their craving for
toys.
All I wanted
And prayed for
Each long waking hour
Was not parties or presents or playthings but power –
I want control
Of every body, every mind, and every soul.
I must dictate,
No number two, that just won't do, no lifetime mate –
Whilst other men gaze at her in a vain attempt to
please,
Why should I fawn and flatter? I require her on her
knees –

76

And I demand
That I have servants who will leap at my command.
Your churchified inanity deserves my full contempt,
Don't preach about humanity to me, I am exempt –
And what is more,
Above the law!

Since I was a boy, how I longed for the day . . .
I could cast all the trappings of childhood away
I can honestly say that my life first began
When the crowd deeply bowed and declared me a man
And I knew as
They knelt, saw
Them cringe and then cower,
(*growing weaker*) No more parties or presents or
    playthings just powe . . .

He fails to reach the final high note.

Oh! The devil take this poison! How can I – not reach –
the – last – note?

Dedrick dies. Albern goes and kneels beside him.

Albern My son? My son? (*looking up*) My son is dead.
(*to Orvin*) You are now the victor. Under the rules –
though it breaks my very heart to say it – you may claim
the hand of my daughter . . .

Orvin (*a bit shaken by all this*) It's alright – if you'd
rather I didn't, I –

Albern Claim her! She's yours!

Orvin No, listen. I don't wish to intrude on your grief at
this time –

Albern (*trembling with rage*) CLAIM HER! YOU
MURDERING FIEND!

Orvin (*placating him*) Right! Right! Just as you like!

Orvin goes to the throne and stands in front of Delcine.

Archbishop (*softly*)
I in my turn do pledge myself to thee, fair one. Arise!

Orvin
I in my turn do pledge myself to thee, fair one. Arise!

He attempts to help Delcine to her feet. Instead she falls forward off the throne and lands at his feet.

(*jumping back in alarm*) Wah! (*examining the knife mechanism*) Well, just look at that, then!

Courtier Look to the Princess!

Albern has witnessed this with horror.

Albern (*grabbing up Dedrick's sword, apoplectic*)
You . . . you . . . you . . .

He lurches a couple of steps in Orvin's direction, staggers, drops the sword, falls to his knees.

My curse upon you – Oswald!

Albern dies.

Courtier Look to the King!

No one moves. Orvin stands, ringed by corpses.

Orvin I – er . . . I – I – well . . . Yes.

A shocked silence.

Asphodel What have you *done*?

Orvin It wasn't me!

Women What have you *done*?

Orvin Look, all I – All I –? (*appealing to Ola*) Didn't I –? That's all I – Tell them.

Ola (*mystified*) Who are you talking to?

Orvin Oh, for goodness' sake!

Griswold Well it can't end like this.

Hilliard It certainly can't.

Ingmar We need an ending.

Junius A proper ending.

Women Hear! Hear!

Kenrick
Meeting.

Disa
Better have a meeting.

Lathrop
Meeting time!

Men
Meeting time!

Women
Meeting time!

Chorus
Meeting time!

Orvin (*over this last*) Oh no, not again!

The Chorus all assemble as before in a huddle. Orvin watches them resignedly.

Asphodel
Mutter . . . mutter . . . mutter . . . mutter . . . (*etc.*)

Berengaria
(*with her*)
Mumble . . . mumble . . . mumble . . . mumble . . . (*etc.*)

Calista (*with them*)
Chatter . . . chatter . . . chatter . . . chatter . . . (*etc.*)

Disa (*with them*)
Murmur . . . murmur . . . murmur . . . murmur . . .
(*etc.*)

Elva (*with them*)
Talky . . . talky . . . talky . . . talky . . . (*etc.*)

Flavia (*with them*)
Conversation . . . conversation . . . conversation . . . (*etc.*)

Griswold (*with them*)
Point of order . . . point of order . . . (*etc.*)

Hilliard (*with them*)
Objection . . . objection . . . objection . . . (*etc.*)

Ingmar (*with them*)
I propose we . . . I propose we . . . (*etc.*)

Junius (*with them*)
I second that . . . I second that . . . I second that . . .
(*etc.*)

Kenrick (*with them*)
All in favour? . . . All in favour? . . . All in favour? . . .
(*etc.*)

Lathrop (*with them*)
Those against? . . . Those against? . . . Those against?
(*etc.*)

Chorus (*in unison*)
Agreed!

The Chorus return to their seats.

Orvin So what have you decided? No, please don't tell
me . . .

Asphodel We have a new ending!

Lathrop A new ending!

Chorus
> And so it came about that brave Ulmar slew the
> enemies of Sollistis –
> And the people rejoiced!
> Rejoiced!
> Rejoiced!
> Crying –
> Long live the King!
> Long live the King!
> Long live the Queen!
> Long live the –

*They break off for a moment as they realise that
Orvin currently has no queen.*

Orvin (*grabbing Ola*) Come on then!

Ola (*startled*) What?

Orvin You'll do!

Chorus (*resuming again happily*)
> Long live the Queen!

*The onstage characters, led by the Archbishop, now
dress Orvin and Ola in regal robes and perform a
double coronation. Orvin puts up with it reluctantly
whilst Ola is completely dazed. During this the
Chorus sing a sort of Coronation Anthem.*

> Carpe diem,
> Bona fide,
> Panem et circenses,
> Ne plus ultra,
> Nota bene,
> In loco parentis.
> Caveat emptor,
> Prima facie,
> Reductio ad absurdum.
> Mea culpa,

In extremis.
Sic transit gloria mundi,
Et tu Brute,
Compos mentis,
Ex officio,
Ex Cathedra,
Ex parte,
Mutatis mutandis,
Etcetera! Etcetera! Etcetera!

As this ends, the crowd have knelt, heads bowed.
Only Orvin and Ola are left standing.
   Silence.

Orvin
   And the King . . .

Ola
   And the Queen . . .

Orvin
   They counted to ten –

Ola
   Then they both held their breath –

   They both start to move off.

Orvin
   As they tip-toed away . . .

Both
   And were never seen in this place –
   Again!

   They both rush off.

Courtier Look to the happy couple!

Chorus (*indignantly*) Where have they gone?

Lathrop That's not the ending!

Asphodel The legend cannot end like this.

Griswold Nor will it. We will write the end as it will be –

Lathrop – as it should be!

Berengaria The end of the legend –

Hilliard – of Orvin –

Calista – and Ola is written thus:

Ingmar Ola and Orvin finally returned to the City of Zeva –

Disa – where, upon their arrival –

Flavia – there were great celebrations –

> *The courtiers, including the 'dead', are transformed into a merry rollicking crowd.*
> *Jolly music to match this.*

Junius – for there was peace for the first time in over one hundred years.

Elva And the Mayor of Zeva addressed the people:

> *Music stops. The crowd quieten.*

Mayor Friends and citizens! This is a momentous day! To celebrate this, it has been decreed that the old town clock which has stood on this site for ninety years, symbolising the hatred and enmity between our peoples, should this day be destroyed! But eventually, in –

Man Shame!

Mayor Wait! Wait! But eventually, in due course, in its place – there will be a new clock built, representing the peace and harmony and love brought about by our two great heroes, Orvin and Ola!

> *Cheers. Music resumes. More merriment.*

Chorus
    So it was,
    That Orvin and Ola lived happily in Zeva,
    Heroes for the rest of their long days.

Men
    And finally, when they died in each other's arms,

Women
    Aged one hundred and five,

Chorus
    The new clock was finally built.
    And the couple were remembered by everyone
    With love in their hearts,
    For ever!

    *Whirring sound as before. Close down to the clock
    again. This time it is Orvin and Ola, or their
    representations, that enter from different sides. They
    come together jerkily and, as they kiss, the clock
    strikes twelve. The lights start to fade during this till,
    on the last strike:*

Griswold That's the ending . . .

Chorus Yes, that's the *end*.

    *And there is a
        Blackout.*

    End.